A Legacy of Birds

A Legacy of Birds

poems by

Sharon Perkins Ackerman

© 2025 Sharon Perkins Ackerman. All rights reserved.
This material may not be reproduced in any form, published,
reprinted, recorded, performed, broadcast,
rewritten, or redistributed without
the explicit permission of Sharon Perkins Ackerman.
All such actions are strictly prohibited by law.

Cover design by Shay Culligan
Cover photo by Ralph Mayhew on Unsplash
Author photo by Sharon P. Ackerman

ISBN: 978-1-63980-688-1

Kelsay Books
502 South 1040 East, A-119
American Fork, Utah 84003
Kelsaybooks.com

For my father

Acknowledgments

These poems have appeared in the following journals:

Appalachian Places: "All Our Histories," "Heritage," "The Field," "The Morning My Father Is Buried"
Meridian: "Tomatoes"
Southern Humanities Review: "A Walk After Retirement"
Still: The Journal: "Willie Nelson Back When," "Winter Nuthatches," Jephthah's Daughter," "Copperhead on the Sidewalk"
Streetlight Magazine: "From Ice and Dust"
Valparaiso Poetry Review: "Point Vierge"

Contents

Winter Nuthatches	15
The Field	16
A Walk After Retirement	17
Song	18
A Legacy of Birds	19
Goblets	20
Winter Flowers	21
Point Vierge	22
Consider the Lilies of the Field	23
Heritage	24
Vespers	25
The Edge	26
The Garden	27
Days When I Want It Back	28
Stars	29
Persimmon Tree	30
Tomatoes	31
Grosbeak in Early Spring	32
Nelson County Hurricane	33
Pilgrimage	34
Red-Shouldered Hawk	35
The Donkey at Stony Point	36
Unconsecrated	37
Black Water	38
When Mountains Fall Away	39
Katydid	40
Full Sturgeon Moon	41
Roots	42
Of River and Shore	43
Market Days	44
Mars	45
Mailbox Route 748	46
Old Friends	47

Hurricane Season	48
Just Before Hard Winter	49
Root Cellar	50
Vernal Equinox	51
From the field at night,	52
Willie Nelson Back When	53
Last Fall Days in the Schoolyard	54
At Twenty on the Banks of the Holston	55
An Abandoned Farm in Virginia	56
Cade's Cove at Midnight	57
You ought to find yourself a little white church,	58
Rain Journal in a Time of Absence	59
A Farewell	60
In Early Spring	61
Locus	62
Appalachian Migration, 1964	63
Matins	64
Full Moon	65
The Web	66
Great Horned Owl	67
Iron Skillet	68
Warm in the Sun	69
Somewhere Near Harlan	70
Remember Lot's Wife	71
Mythical Eagle Redux	72
Bracelet	73
Dead Coyote	74
Midnight, December Solstice	75
Autumn Geese	76
Jephthah's Daughter	77
Stony Point	78
At Two Years	79
Stack Cake	80

Planting in December	81
Copperhead on the Sidewalk	82
All Our Histories	83
Fall's Labor, Fall's Memory	84
Morning After Rain	85
Winter Vultures	86
The Morning My Father Is Buried	87
From Ice and Dust	88
Blackbird Days	89

"The last time I beheld
That scarlet and black
Sumptuous bird
Was when I moved into
This house by the sea
Twenty years ago.
He flew to the flowering
Andromeda."

—May Sarton. "Birthday Present." In *Coming Into Eighty*.
  W.W. Norton & Company, 1994. P. 69

Winter Nuthatches

In late afternoon as water blackens,
crusts in low-lying pools
a nuthatch calls, hardening
the trees for night, answered
by a faint echo up the hill.
They've found each other
across spaces of cold, voices
cracked like ice, as air between
them carries the immeasurable—
How light on a pond
seems a long ways away,
how when you walk toward a mountain
it moves back. Always, the mimicry
and mirage of distances,
the folly of believing this life might
never end, cord between body
and earth someday dissolved.
I can't see the striped heads
but I hear them stitching
the line between themselves
bough to bough, together again
just before dark.

The Field

It's sweet how goldenrod waits
        at the end of summer
                milkweed unscrolling its husks,

tithing seeds. In just a few weeks
nettle will snap in umber
                tones underfoot, a low flame light

the field where flights of swallows turn
        themselves loose at sunset,
                bodies near as they pass,

yet muted. They don't understand
        even now, their own distances,
                old love, the ache of it.

A Walk After Retirement

Sun falls in sheaves on pine,
drips to gold pools
molten at the Equinox.
Otherwise, it's wingstem

head-high, reflection wavered
in the river. Pollinators
worry stalks and I leave them alone,
no longer inclined to test

the temperaments of this world.
Still there's a moment—
a web brushed away, a gentle
stick sparing the spider.

Only last week a bear cub
trotted its new courage
over the bright leaves before me.
Do no harm,

the young woman promised 35 years ago,
adjusting green scrubs
in the mirror, but that's not
the way an animal travels

through its hungers. *I'll keep trying,*
I whisper to the shade
as it moves alone, changing
its lines, blessing what it can.

Song

At fifteen I dreamed once
I was dying,
relieved to wake in sheets
damp with hormones,
hyacinth floating in the window,
the limbs, the tongue
curious again, my mother's footstep
in the hall.
One day, I thought
one day, as the junco
a mile away piped in scales
above the surface
of the world
and my body turned
back to itself and sang.

A Legacy of Birds

A cry of wood thrush bells glass
down streams, breaks the water,

sky and leaves, shattered delicacies
a foraging eye might reassemble.

I don't recall the forest's foodways
as my mother did, maybe wood sorrel

or dandelion, bright shoots to fill days
when salted meat subdivides to zero,

or a chest cold begs tonic. Rounded
in tiny fungi, bark sheds its memory

to damp shelves that never dry out,
frilled and fringing pine. While threaded

through fern, the blackbird's account
of faces, the old cabin of ancestors

where I pause, a wedge of rotted rail
in hand, parsing songs that climb

ruined joists as pole beans in sun's shrill
glare, still green, still young.

Goblets

I always forget the name
...... *chesapeake*
where we bought wine goblets,

rich reds our favorite for Fridays.
In between days,
austere in cupboards, they learn

to sit still, hold a certain pose
in dry times
curtained off from summer tables

to float in storage bays later,
hard fronts
glinting at strange noises as rain

beats on metal doors.
I packed our split in newspaper,
called it every kind

of failure, but two of four glasses
survive, clean-lined
in cabinets, smoothed

in symmetries a human face
uses to hide pain. In the darkness,
each one keeps its shape.

Winter Flowers

My grandfather died digging coal
at thirty-three. Before he went,
he held up each of his seven
children and told them goodbye.
What he said, only they know
sealed over like snowdrops
in cold, damp solitudes.
Some stories call out past the river,
only to rest in cicada-wasted
leaves, cobwebbed in trees.
Along low banks, the houses
of my people sleep. Words when they come,
bring winter flowers
kicking up mud out of nowhere.

Point Vierge

It's the kind of February morning

where a full moon not quite set
warms in sparks of nascent sun

and you shiver through chores
bearing birdseed door to feeder.

Close, then closer, the inchoate
day forms clay-like in branches,

light gullies over the frozen call
of a raven, posed on the trellis

of a dead tree, his tenuous hold
and loud hiccups charcoaling sky.

In his racket, there's what you know
and what you don't know

of any presence uttering your name
—Or how it might be answered

but to enter the world through cold
clouds, choosing all over again.

Consider the Lilies of the Field

In late September, a cool snap
means soup, the garden yield of herbs
reaped for the pot. Thyme,
oregano, parsley culled from beds
of still-blooming beebalm,
while acorns fall beside scolding squirrels,
and sun blisters then whips
the birds south on belts of wind.
A time to keep, a time to cast away,
but here, this gray in-between,
where I've been before, unsure
of what to do. Was it always like this—
harvest and lingering green,
hummingbirds begging nectar in the chill?
How long they need feeding
is a mystery, a crapshoot, invisible
shifting almanac of air.
There are days I feed and days I stop.
Stand smack in the middle
of toil and spin. Listen to a red
woodpecker excavate his hole,
pecking away, bright, holy fool
of the garden, still working it all out

Heritage

You don't know what you're made of to start,
so many things run in the blood
a looseness of limb
quiet from a long line of quiet.

The brine of a river in the hair
means *born,* one name flowing
into another, inked cursive
in a bible that says come or be summoned.

I'm baptized because my daddy
believed in the brown leaf
smell of water, loading his child's pockets
with the living and the dead,

so the streams bore that weight.
Wade out on silt and it begins to exhale
below your feet. I felt it once—
my mouth flooded by something lighter than love.

Vespers

There is no exact word
for what birds do as they descend
sky to low shrub

pushing air until
it hums differently
like two soft gloves rubbed together.

The bones of a wing
are hollow, night-ready
for the light tread of braille

which rights our lives as it will,
dusk loosening its glitter
over a border of maple.

See how every darkness is made
of crazy starlings
mixing up the breeze,

black feathers sparking round
in opposite directions—
their great change of heart.

The Edge

The first time I see the ocean
it is taller than me,
dolphins horsing around
on light-limned waves
that gobble and spit.
A fat kid waves a mandible
fresh combed in his bucket,
foam glosses a severed claw.
Seas of burned faces
cling to this fragmentary place
whose smoke-tinted fish
creak warnings of promising time
to each other or even ourselves.
Look to the edge, a gull cries
as the story of my life undocks
its hull scraping the beach
a white, white sail
visible for a time, then not.

The Garden

Spring planting is habit
bestowed, a woman walking
at dusk to her garden, hat brim
frayed in fingerprints,
grass worn as testament
to the usefulness of paths in life.
I go out again, seeds and hoe
as I went last year, as I was taught—
to break ground in silence
letting corn tassels spark in sun,
pole beans and squash
left to their quirks, trailing as they
please in serpentine rows. Knowing
the shapes they can become,
I wish in ripening, for straighter
certainties. My hands push
soil, rooting down to the first
grandmother in this country,
her curled vines I've let stretch
under a lazy sun. Fresh nubs
grow on last season's tendril,
shoots tendered from wintering,
new green growth
that comes on top of old. When we say
grace later, we mean this.

Days When I Want It Back

From dirt . . . . . . to dirt they return,
acorns, the cranefly
who dances on black leaves,
the thud of apples rolling
back to the underworld.
One day at fifty,
my courses just stopped,
leaving the blood red sumac
to hold its place in the field.

Stars

It was the gods who placed them in frozen
frames, so the Greeks thought.
light speeding backwards in endless telling.

Hung on that skein of time,
my mother sits young on the moonless porch,
telling family stories,

hickory-scented chapters of endless lines;
coal lines, picket lines, school lines,
lines of inheritance,

ten child broods thick as boiling syrup
each of them a constellation
sparking upwards, leading somehow to us.

All we know of the sky
is what she gives us to know, white cotton blouse
swirled down her back

like the milky way, her face a porcelain cup
offered to the dark,
pouring down stars to her children.

Persimmon Tree

It stands in a curve of road
below a knob, as autumn climbs

down, ripens the cotton our tongues
know so well. It takes time

for a dream to sweeten
and what has been realized

over these fifty years, who can say?
All summer the tree disguises

itself as Godly things do,
but in November the bright-woven

sweaters of children flock round
to its kindling snap and clove

scent. How shall they learn
of harvest in their unharrowed

days, but to find branched,
the saddle-shaped notches burrowed

so a shoe can climb up and up
until the soul hears the tree ringed

by orange flame, call back the birds,
thrush and jay, starlings

careening down. *Eat,* it says
and they do. *Now, sing!*

Tomatoes

Eight tomatoes across twelve plants
—harder now to spark
than in earlier years.
Yet a cloud of bees filtered in
one morning,
all industry and hope,
praised blossom to blossom
the scarcity.

When my grandmother sang,
it was worship—joy moved
through things, fat golden boys
beefsteaks, heirlooms.

I want to ask the yet green globes
how a hand, so familiar
still moves in mystery
between rows. To weep
as their skins,
translucent in direct light,
reveal themselves
as a child's face will
clean through to the seeds.

Grosbeak in Early Spring

Rose patch.
Flash.
Suddenly in days of cardboard
one moment collapsed
into another,
the grosbeak streaks to a perch
loosening the sky
of cloud-layered memory.
It takes years to forget
what love's entry feels like
to the eye, the skin,
synesthesia; hand listening,
eye blinded. We meet again,
you who've come
as refugee to a warmer place.
You who were once
scarlet in a sea of sparrows,
who took the chance
of being beautiful
against all that brown.

Nelson County Hurricane

They said it was chance—
that odd crease in the space
around our bodies, we don't
question until later.
Dark clouds roiled the valley
but it was only rain predicted
so we brought in clothes

off the line. Who knew?
Might as well question the mustard seed,
its tiny infinite spark.
Twenty-seven inches of water
a *theoretical maximum,*
weather scientists would say
but in the end, it was that apple

found near Davis Creek
after Camille tore down mountains
and left the Ginger Gold
gleaming above water. A sweet yellow
sun to mock the mudslide,
parentage of two or three fragments,
a tree that would never have been,

grafted for no good reason
on the back of the wind.

Pilgrimage

If you walk alone in deep russet
woods, blacken your phone
carry the creed you've written so it rests
against a thigh, sparingly known
shy as a fern. Can you proclaim
the yellow wing-stem, find enchanted
the notches of leaves so lightly named
—Is your own name thus slanted?
In time a body takes the shape given
to wanderers, the self sewn
to its six-foot stem, no longer riven
by wind, fluttering with no due remittance.
Child, imagine that box of sin you carried across
each acre of life, filled now with moss.

Red-Shouldered Hawk

Above a fork of poplar
his *kee-yah*

confirms
there is a time to dance
a time to cry out

for the field mouse astir
in autumn grass, for a knee

bent in solitude.   Why not waltz
the sky, holding the dead
closer than any grave?

There must be a way to carry
that which no longer lives,

that which we miss terribly,
beyond earthly balm.

I've seen the hawk circle
for miles and miles
rusted wings beating away

until the memory of one life
vanishes inside another,
becomes the scratch

against the sky, then the speck
and then gone.

The Donkey at Stony Point

He lives by the house
that used to be White's Store
and the post office,

by a road that used to be
called Coursey's road.
And people who remember that,

also tell of an old corn mill
diagonal to the field
tucked to a curve so drivers

slow cars as the donkey
walks the loop of his run
back and forth. *Lomp, clomp!*

Slight head bob, his nod
to the usefulness of a path
in life, routines that hold

our place when we cannot love
this alien world. Sometimes
under the stone of a moon

the beast forgets how to turn
around, lowers his forehead
to the fence and pushes.

Unconsecrated

It's a particular human foolishness
that makes a truck's tin plates
more than they are—
Now that body and engine are gone,
hauled to a parts salvage
their numbers and letters
identifiers of twenty years,
spell out the spry days
of squashing furniture and feed
into the bed. In its time it hauled
a succession of dogs
smelling out the side window
as rust slow-pocked its hood.
All the flowers and shrubs
I ever planted, rode in on it,
became all they could be
in the quickening of summer.
The front plate is nailed
to a tree off in the woods now.
Unconsecrated, free to haunt
any passing hunter,
shining like sulfur on a night
when the moon hits it just right.

Black Water

Sometimes the water gets tired of flowing
and pools some place low
where apples fall, hornets kissing sugar
off sweet rot. One day it lets
scant rain put it to bed, dammed
in leaves and sticks, a round, dark dime
shining its singularity at the bottom
of a ravine. I've seen coal hauled
to surface lighter than forsaken
streams, the tar mirror where nothing lives,
everything reflects its night
image. Trees loom, full of shadows
and I ask you if there is beauty
even here, if stars when they grace
such stagnant space, still penetrate,
holding our gaze in utter sacrilege.

When Mountains Fall Away

When there is nothing left to say
I will stare out to limestone cliffs
risen from salt, the hawk's sway
born of an old sea shimmy and drift.

I'll know my grandmother's gaze
like a captain's wife sighting nests
of eagles from her porch, her gray
eye, my brown one, skirting a crest

of pine, its wilderness of psalms
treading waters. When words cease,
dry banks will spread open their palms,
our silence lodging in creases

of remembered rivers, bedrock's cleft—
Listening, finally, will be what is left.

Katydid

I should have doused the light
before she caught
half-bodied in the door, flight
startled, flat pea pod
wings glistening on the deck.
They say her song brings in winter,
the season my father lay
in casket and I noticed for the first
time, his smallish, tapered hands.
But the katydid placed in a leaf,
thin legs kicking at the moon,
confesses the fragility
of things that lie wrong in the mind,
a flutter in the dark, stillness
after a clumsy arc. Then snow
and snow and snow, covering
the green that glows deep,
unbeknown, like mint out of season.

Full Sturgeon Moon

What does the leaping fish
feel? Is it surprise—
*Why, I'm as limber
as a young woman,*
remembering the form
he once saw kicking above.

It's just like love, isn't it,
to wreak terror on moonlight
as August ripples by,
breaking seven feet
into the air, suspended briefly
where it can't survive.

Roots

Who knows what makes a body
stay or leave a place—
Peace can be simple, light's infusion
along a wild reed of use to no one.

All over this acreage
milkweed spills white seeds
in feathered wings on the ground,
its best angel given

to one spot. Sometimes it's like this;

you run a finger along
the horizon of a square field
and its frame opens to blue
infinity. Until one day your song

barely causes the wrens to shift
in their nests. You,
the accidental sprout,
you the myth.

Of River and Shore

There are hours the river belongs
to its mirror
and nothing else, when fixed
in the glass, laurel's five-pointed

star shines on pinwheels
of trillium, a still-life pierced
by the blue-gray heron's step
as it cracks the mirror, pieces it back.

Nothing stays shattered;
damselflies, a rubyspot or rainbow—
chimera skating the shallows
of ancestral memory, clouds

of faces, now fat
now thin, floating virescent
out of touch. There are ways of being
in the water I've yet to know; skimmers,

skippers, gliders, heat-lit energies
threaded in wings. Far off gravestones
cry concrete tears, but here
moss banks hold our vacancies,

waves lift seeming solidities,
dislodge driftwood so it breaks again.
Rafting past burrowed squirmers,
who see up through the darkly

glass, past minnow and mollusk,
this body's newly loosed fragment
sailing surfaces of light. Not the whole
of it perhaps, but a part.

Market Days

I wish I'd kept my shopping lists
from two decades ago
blurred dollars and cents
counting back to Friday afternoons
walking to the vegetable stand.
My summer dress unravels
from thread-worn memory;
corn perking up from sacks,
the way rainbow chard
climbs out of its wrapping,
damp against your hand.
I guess it's not so much
the prices and balances

that want for reconciliation,
but what isn't recalled in coinage—
How the scent of boxwood
crowds a sidewalk, or light
finds its way under eaves
late day as you pass by,
the heft of strawberries
and melon unsettling both arms.
How it feels to release them
heat-cramped to a cool counter
mid-noon, as the morning glory
loses its crown
and trucks slam away.

Mars

You are positioned left
        of the tallest maple,

not exactly a celestial
        increment, but one that pastes

you to a place
        the naked gaze can find.

Consider bug-eyed men,
        lasers shot from saucers,

stray spark of summer bonfires
        the color a scraped knee

oozes. Peachier than other bodies,
        you blush among the dead

drawing the eye to imagined
        water, algae, single cells,

always the light we call to
        from coordinates of lawn chairs

and marshmallow sticks.
        What is the warm evening

then, family on blankets in grass,
        but a brief glance

toward skies full of things
        we cannot touch, or childhood

but the longest, greenest memory
        of hoping for life.

Mailbox Route 748

Cast metal clicks in heat
a domed oven so you half expect
a loaf of bread to pop out.
There's MAIL in raised letters,
the basket of sunflowers

at its base a victory over time
and distance.
Leave the door flapped open
and a wren's nest appears
incubating the long series of days

spent running down a drive
to find a surprise package
hanging out the end, or a note—
See you this summer.
Most days the box waits the way

you wait down a silent hall
of missing another—clock-heavy, a stone
in each pocket.   *Oh Grandmothers,*
imagine the letters we could write
now, each of us old,

the postman's hand spiriting
spaces between us, our stories
flying wing to wing,
falling fine as cotton handkerchiefs
on your porches.

Old Friends

My friends have crossed
over. The ones who assembled
in mountain overhangs
in rain, came with a gas can
when my car ran empty,
knew what it meant to tremble
in cold diesel at a truck stop.
You were my first family
after family, the six pack
starter beer, the dash-light
confessional. The kin I've
lit a candle for, remembered
over a blush wine
when I peel shrimp to boil.
Pink-fleshed, shells so itinerant
and thin, they slip off,
wandering the counter in twilight.

Hurricane Season

Hurricane rain is the only kind
we get this time of year,
bluster straying inland until it butts
up to mountains, calm eye
where autumn hides in clouds
prowling in dark silhouettes.
The wind throws hints, kicks dust
at footprints, the patches
of ground where nothing grows.
Like deer, we leave flattened
grass behind, signatures on parched,
papery earth that offer up
to coming storms, the soft hills

of our bodies teased by a gray
sense of arrival. As if breezes
in their theft of light—stored
all summer in crabapples and peaches,
might leave our golden reason
for being here, burning in the trees.

Just Before Hard Winter

Leaves hang in copper coils,
cardinals pick up speed
in the flash of days. We're always
reminding each other
how quickly it gets dark,
as if life is now a circle of sun
to be chased around,

faces tilted to the last ray
before extinction. A few miles
over our heads, air ceases
to hold the tiniest lung,
turns blood pure blue, the heart's
frozen lake. Any winged
ambitions we replace with fire,

creatures in the dry caves
of our homes who'd rather burn
than freeze. Chimneys smoke
with our earthbound flames,
licking up toward eternities
of dead stars— this warmth
between us, all that we have.

Root Cellar

Under my grandma's high porch,
cooler than leaves, I hear
rockers creek on the floor

above, voices soft like spiders
knitting at dusk. What I'll recall
is the door's webbed eave,

its easy push from light
to dark. And the way shade enters
a soul—through a dirt floor

chilling bare feet, snakeskins
strung over apple bins,
rafters where a moon ought to hang

and doesn't. Sometimes it's all
about blackness; tubers and roots
dungeoned, things that grow

more of themselves, lunar eyes
of potatoes, onions sprouting green.
Curing, adults say and I know

they listen for me down here
by the sweet pickles, jars of yellow
peaches glinting like suns.

Nothing to see down there but dust,
they say, but each year
I descend the stairs, prowl smells

of damp rot, fruit preserves shining
in a tomb of lumber that has not, not yet, given way.

Vernal Equinox

Despite this burgeoning
the periphery holds;
how nicely the world obliges
new petals, the green shove
insisting on itself
first, above all. Beautiful.

Soon cherry blossoms will mock
the dead, the season fight
for its young, as from the beginning
of time, the weakest pup
edged off the breast
      —I want my milk! Such bald

fierceness locks into place
the tenderest shoot,
drills through hardened clay
and sidewalk, every crack
unfurls a fresh minted flower's
capacity for surprise.

I thought I was done with love—
but no, it all comes back doesn't it?
Just as Spring bends on one knee
offering emeralds.

From the field at night,

Orion struts his dogs in perpetuity,
dwarfs and giants cluster
in colonies of aliases like Sirius
and Lyra, luminous ghosts
from a long extinct luster.

The sky I've understood so little of
boils bright between clouds
crowded and burning as ever,
always some nebula
churning up a black unknown,

questions of whether this life
might have been more than,
or larger. But this fraction
I stand upon offers a gleaming
thread of flesh; breath of peepers,

crickets ruffling night grasses
geese shining as heat lightning
flashes over the pond—
And the human form,
face tilted up in a field, would stars

be part of her smallness, or she
a part of their scale, as they ache
inside her throat, calling
to be named out of darkness
into sharp, solitary blades of light.

Willie Nelson Back When

It would be years before I'd smoke
his seeds of redemption
but at seven all the lyrics
of River Boy rowed off my tongue.

A child sings because she can,
a lament no more aware
than a flatboat's low passage
dragonflies dredging sunlight at its edge.

My daddy grew up on the waters
of Kentucky, bringing its rhythms
into our house, his turntable
and humming, my hands

unconscious rhyme, sloshing
through chores. Mostly mournful
stuff, doves at dusk cooing
back their lot—*This old world*

don't hold a whole lotta joy—
our bond of muscle memory,
when the fishing line snapped
loose from its lapping tunes,

my father's open casket.
Me the adult, stiff as a swimmer
braced for the cold depths.

Last Fall Days in the Schoolyard

It's the scratch of wool
that perturbs, best friends
perched like nuthatches
in black and white jumpers

on a concrete slab, far corner
of the schoolyard. Low country
we've claimed, stippled
in oak, we might be birds

unused to the itch of fabric,
linked by wings and chatter.
It seems now, even the breeze
pries us from leaves,

acorn-dusted, driving a stick in dirt
as burial mound. When the class
bell rings, we walk on gold.
The wind cries the way a baby cries.

At Twenty on the Banks of the Holston

A fishing line hauls up
the moon, a tug whose tension

we barely feel, banked on light
blankets. We keep still,

our reflections hold place
like foam on the green shoots

pooling until it froths away.
How long we'll sit here

I can't say; the horizon's hemline
darkens in water. Boats pass.

There are forces we can't begin
to understand, runnels

cleaving the breastbone
that from one angle, fills,

another, empties. What can we
do but watch night fire up

point by point in the river,
shed clothes and dust in its new

star mirror—Able swimmers,
scions yet, of streams.

An Abandoned Farm in Virginia

Gravel makes a sound more solemn
than silence, a dream of cottages,
horses field-grazing, kept by columns
of oak. *Hayground* one is named,

for its old labors. Nothing moves,
no breeze to rattle a stand of dry
thistle, spent heads hung in full moons
as they travel their fencerow

in and out of form. The main house
stares downcast, door propped a crack
so if we care to, we can browse
cylinder glass, query fieldstone

on how a room empties one day,
the great truth of its life taken back.
As though to bear us away,
sunlight paints a ladder on the walls.

Cade's Cove at Midnight

Rooftops of the old settlement
gleam like a steel shovel.
Legend tells that otters
once played in its streams
but this night, just the glide
of three teenagers
edging their way into darkness.
We do not know yet
the blood of history rowing in us,
that our stories weave
into whispers of sleeping
spirits, forms blended
past-present, no more than shadows
along the split rail. Slowly,
the tune of a nightjar's
serenade silvers the grass
where I watch you watching her
as she watches the moon—
We believe this ache to be our own.

You ought to find yourself a little white church,

my daddy tells me—
himself a product of eight generations
of lay ministers riding bareback
along the Kentucky river.
What he means is all that
blood fervor will hoof its way
across any stream to lay
the first block of foundation
for a long room of dust—
A place that stands quiet
most of the time, nave
bathed in lemon oil sheen
pools of sun crossing themselves
at its alter, coming to kneel
before a slatted hymnal board,
caught in week-long shadows
between reaping and song.
He means that if you enter
there enough Sunday mornings
you'll eventually hear
in pine planks creaking
beneath your light-bound feet,
something tall and dark.

Rain Journal in a Time of Absence

I've pared the garden
to meet water's breakage,
pried tomatoes
from bruising sludge,
memory twisting around itself
in damp braids as it muses
on faces missing or gone.
It's the memorial of hands in dirt
low acreage stranded
in dramas of detritus or age,
crows who play back
what's forgotten; reflections
of a younger woman
fast-moving as a cloud
across pools of rising bogs
where the glassy dead swim
shoulder to shoulder.
Near my knees on burlap
new tendrils curl their voices,
query cardinals who answer
by doing again what they did
before: Spilling down in red
ecstasy,
singing
wet-mouthed, thriving in ruin.

A Farewell

Threshold of summer's leaving,
hay bales wait in wheels as skies
match-struck, burn off a three
month haze in blue flame.
Though much is on the move
in September, rolled grain and grasses
pause on bobbins, circumspect,
holding reels of sun. Out of that
brightness, comes thunder,
flatbeds to load umber spools
of old histories packed tight.
And there on swept pastures,
used to such refractions of light,
our bodies face each other again
as the field is hauled away.
Gold straw bound for mouths
of lambs, the driver a stranger
whose tanned arm waves and waves
as he turns onto the highway.

In Early Spring

On the walk I touch everything,
new nubs of pinecones in sockets,
winter wheat shining
waxen at fingertips, bud clusters
held to the lips like cold wine.
How friable, petals and peels
of bark, how suspicious the fresh
thorns! Last fall I held
a frozen trowel in my hand
and watched green
drain back down a stalk,
like a whistling pot boiling to nothing,
and knew I'd misunderstood time,
its vault of buried seeds.

Locus

I get lost so easily,
fifty cars
in a parking lot, same color.

Or worse—
fall leaves masking a path,
what dirt used to look
like, leading home.

I forgive the adolescent
then, her blurred body
sifting red and gold
for some final form,

days she can't recall
the walking
or even how light
scatters motes

in no pattern. That she'll forget
the stray bounce of her hair,
her limbs dividing the air
into here and gone.

Appalachian Migration, 1964

At age seven I don't understand
why the river through Louisville
is named the Ohio.
I believe its bridge is a steel insect,
jaws at both ends,

teeth that divide air and grass
between the place I live
and the place I'm home.
I have not learned to throw my arms
open to such spaces yet,

where cables of miles
landscape the body into exile.
Better to count the curves to my grandma's
house, past the vast waters
to coves of faces I memorize;

Uncle Ray, Beck, Big Bill, and Zolie.
My little coal-eyed girl, a cousin
calls, naming me like the dishes of chicken,
dumplings, sweet corn, and beans
we pass over a table, one shore to another.

Matins

Not I, but this.
Each of us, a wave in the surge,
our faces half a sphere

dark, full of what will happen
and hasn't yet.
As children we supposed things,

morning's brush tugged the hair
rough as field flowers,
light brooked our curtains

grabbed a shoulder, shook us out
onto grass. Even the best
of us have forgotten

the blue jay's bark, or mistaken
its hallelujah
for loneliness. Oh, to return

to such swimming and air
as if we might speak one
intelligible word

to the watery morning.
As if *happy* is the sun
breaking water in a gasp.

Full Moon

You can see the whole of it now
no black clouds to tie knots
across the light,
so like the quicksilver
we prodded with fingers
as children. Could it be time

that divides itself, comes together
in one ball only to break
apart again? The important thing
is that a body grows larger
beneath such cycles,
swells with its own fluidity,

never hardening beyond
an expectation of grace. The moon
shines on a fencepost,
a tin roof, the dirt that buries us.
Rolls radiant over the palm,
half death, half magic.

The Web

If I have affinity for a thing,
we will move towards each other,
find the hiding spot no one knows.

As a child, I hid and waited for my father
in a field that grew inside me,
watching a garden spider's design

drift from her sunlit fingers, a yellow
starburst on her mounded back.
What shape can ever replace that

which rose unsummoned and free?
Where the insects tore holes, her legs
stitched it closed. In tall grass, I saw

how the many eyes of this world
rip a life apart, sew it back together.

Great Horned Owl

It isn't a lonesome cry
that plays to dusk
but more a puzzle, a *why*
vibrato pushing a void

the same way the universe moves
or is said to, into nothing.
Staccato then a croon
waltz the tongue of Athena—

but why born of air? It's the womb
that first taught
how the night in bloom
embraces so utterly, a forest.

Where no dim house lays claim,
but stars lit by owls
re-arrange our names,
singing them in the motherless dark.

Iron Skillet

Because her songs banged metal on the stove,
I want to peel
and fry a potato the way my mother did,
crackling in iron—

That black oiled mirror,
where all the faces who made
chimneys smoke with coal, peer back.
Speaking in a soft scrape of spoons,

slow-seasoning this daughter in picked greens
and hog fat. Recalling the beat-stir
rhythm of recipes never written,
passed down in steam and singing

    Now, heat the oven first, then pour the meal
until these wrists feel
the deep digging of ore, one knee in dirt
scouring rust with sand

handles gleaming hand over hand,
blood heavy.
Tender like cornbread that rises over iron,
circular like the sun.

Warm in the Sun

In early March there's a spot
in the yard where shadows do not fall
though they are all around
like the cold, held at bay
high noon, roped off by rays
of gold light. Heavenly light,
first love light. Our camp chairs
planted in a circle of sun,
scoot deeper into its lamp,
away from pewter-edged air.
Imagine a ring of summer,
how two people might lay
newly warm hands on each other
and call it healing. Sleep—
that sparking of sea gulls behind
closed lids as winter exits
and tries to re-enter. Tell me
if you can, who swore us to
this circumference of heat,
older than we ever thought
in our folding seats, tough
with daffodils. Who will say
we are brief as an owl's
breath when the time comes?

Somewhere Near Harlan

My father pulls over and holds me up
to look toward Hoskins Knob.
I ask what the sign says
and he yells, *falling rock zone,*
our voices unable to hold
their own above the gorge's bellow,
swinging bridge loose, cables
honking like geese in fog.
He wants me to see something—
hardwoods of such deep green
they seem black, seas of limbs broken
by coal tipple and shaft, blacker still.
And all the shades of dark; hickory
shells, rain-soaked limestone, moss
and rims of fungus scalloped
roots beside river dross—

What a land of old faith placed
above ground in light, and what was combed
up by force of machine.
Curdled low, smoke clouds roam
mountains in shapes of dragons,
those beasts chained deep in the belly
of the earth, blood and kin
topographies that flow in veins
of someone else's gain.
At night, my father stubs his cigarette
with a shoe and our car cools,
creaking heat to crickets and porch light.
The song of an evening thrush
cuts through air like dynamite.

Remember Lot's Wife

You have to bury a tomato
plant deep, cover
the shoots at base,
snip the lower leaves—
Keeps disease from climbing up.
When I left your house,

mama, moving into
my own, loam rose
over my ankles, I clipped any tendril
that turned toward home.
Salt, I'd say,
remembering the lure

of looking back,
the cankered love for what hurts.
I've taken the worst,
laid that sack of seeds open
to clouds and rain,
one hundred sprouts

wind-stamped, faces following
sun, roots tamped
in rows we've harrowed.
It's a black-eyed bird
that would find any sin here
in the dirt's distant gaze.

Mythical Eagle Redux

When I finally see him, he's low
above the gravel road
over my neighbor's barns
headed toward river cliffs
where I've searched a whole
summer. And here is the thing:
He's all that he's cracked
up to be, breadth of wing
flung to scale, light glinting
off his white head, grace
that unbolted a church door
and flew, flew, flew
along utility poles and rooves—
Shadowing the backs of goats,
green tractors and pines,
the porch where a man
grimaces over a splinter,
the woman shading her eyes
as she reads her letter.
I think it true that the eagle
who passes by, has always been.
Hidden maybe, too high
for recognition, but a design
that holds us plumb,
pulls from a pyre of disbelief,
hope that fledges hollow
inside a palm, waiting for a form to fill it.

Bracelet

Somewhere on the trail
or slightly off
a blue woven bracelet
peeks from glyphs of leaves.

In time, it will prove artifact
of a day remembered or not,
gone from a bright braid
coiling a wrist, to a snake

of color, rain-soiled nibble
of a curious possum or crow.
Woods have taken back
the frayed ends of hemp,

what I thought I could hold
with a knot, warm over
my veins, hides in its state
of unmaking,

loops unfastened to the wind's
purpose. How swiftly a thing
mislaid will lose the shape
assumed for years-

Lost treasures,
lost ambitions, lost love, lost smiles—
The truth is that when we pick them up again,
they are never the same.

Dead Coyote

When I find him, his eyes are closed
lying at a cross of trail
and road as though he fell asleep
after being hit by a car.
Still lithe in death, lovable
even, I'm obliged to visit his corpse
daily as it decomposes.

Vultures descend, then snows,
still his form hovers overhead
in wind, rowdier than usual
howling through window seams
by the bed at night. It must be true,
the myth that coyote once shut
the door on death spirit,

denied entry so grief wanders
outdoors, no relief or limit
to disembodiment. By spring,
only bones thrust up
between buttercups and white clover,
two ivory teeth that I touch,
turn in my palm, and pocket home.

Midnight, December Solstice

Peripheral
where frost ferns the window
clouds skim a low hill
clabbering the darkness.
Sleep with its black wingtip
does not suspect
that across the field
winter has broken its fence,
an albino deer running free.

Autumn Geese

I turn on the porch light
for the night, just as geese fly over,
troubadours filling the deep
with bangled cries, disarming
the darkness with noise.
It's cooler at dusk, the air calmer,
no headwind to tamp out
their flame—That's enough to rejoice,
isn't it? A map, the moon's blaze,
some place off in the distance
waiting up and listening for you.

Jephthah's Daughter

Here is an alphabet of man and garden
a hat brimmed with gospel
born from a land
that would beat a mule to death
if it didn't plow straight.
Do this in remembrance—

I still see you walking down to rows
of trees, spraying the peach
while I cringed, stomping back
a fat cabbage under one arm
It's as big as your head,
grinning.

A daughter's mercies
can frustrate a man,
ours was a battle of soft and hard,
hip broken by an angel
pasture rock for a pillow.
Where there is no clear victor
we call a draw—

In the dream that comes and comes,
you plant tea roses.

Stony Point

There's a crease in the plateau
spread open,
bedrock eased by timothy

mountains
bluing on either side.
A seam that scallops from midpoint,

the time
between first windflowers
and last blackened persimmon,

where the land ever unfolds
or else packs to leave.
What holds the landscape together,

I can't say.
The sun pulls a field of buttercups
up from earth by its own

intention, two horses graze,
facing opposite like bookends,
the meadow equilibrated.

So many stones churn to surface
from a distant buckling
deeper than all blossoms

hard proof that love
does not end here, but tumbles on
the same and utterly changed.

At Two Years

There's a picture of the child
I don't remember
on a blanket in grass
back of a tarpaper house,
slice of red melon in hand
toes waving, face sunny side up.
One palm crams my mouth
plundering sweetness
I can't name and behind
the camera, a mother and father,
nascent shapes in sepia,
creators of an image.
I wonder if I even guessed
from that blank yonder
I was in a body fixing to fly?
Or heard the crow on his eave
above, beak full of sky
snatching spirits from the wind.

Stack Cake

Oldest cake in the mountains:

Apples dried or fresh
      cellar cured
          (even in the dead of winter, most kitchens had them)
          molasses and ginger
          iron pans to hold slabs

of moist spice.
Flour and salt
buttermilk room temperature
cinnamon, cracked walnuts (stored in tins with paper)

And the oven's flame lit
by my mother, heat-blushed
for a moment and shed
of bitter fruit. The girl's
splash of freckles and gray

frock cracking an egg
like her own mother taught her,
one hand caught
in its guilty track, finger
dipped in sweet batter.

Planting in December

Today the corner nursery
closes its season
cinnamon mulling
next to fertilizer, shovels
propped east in hopes
of selling before dark.

It's the markdown bag of irises
I crave,
—or rather the color blue;
sea water, wedgwood,
and high noon blue,
two moons in a month

blue, the bulbs no more
tangible now
than pleated fields, rows
furrowed by absence.
I've tried and failed to love
this season of dips and sags,

knowing the earth
where I'll bed these lumpy children
holds the same dream
as last spring, cellared
in a brine of forgetfulness.
When they are born

into shapes of flowers,
they will already be old,
ready to bear cobalt hues
along a circle
into a land that I call death
and they call *I remember.*

Copperhead on the Sidewalk

You learn in the country
to have your wits about you,
still the snake surprises

on a rare November day
tongue flicking
at a patch of sun. Why not

taste the air—measure
in serpentine scales
what is too easily hidden?

Malice has one tang, prey
another, the human heart
a blade of cruel and kind,

never knowing which end
of the rake will suffice.
Maybe the world is relearned

this way, taking in the savor
of autumn's end,
licking along the navy rim

of evening for danger.
Can we know—ever really,
if it's snake or angel

that clings to the warm cement
tan muscles flexed to defend
every forkful of light.

All Our Histories

There's a picture of my grandma
at seventeen, skin like sweet milk
her eyes so very wise
full of canning and floods, every
kind of venom a mountain can muster.
Looking at her is a kind of loneliness,
like the miles between towns
or the overhang view of a valley
where you can see how a river runs
but it's too far off to swim.
There was a husband she loved
who died young, done in by coal mines
or a bad heart, twin truths
flowing side by side. Another man
who may have been bad—or not,
who she may have married,
or not. And in time, ten children
jumping the banks, wet filaments
spreading north. But this is the girl
before, who cannot disclose
what she doesn't know yet.
Old stories will come from high up
and later, from many directions
so they can't be told apart,
but like haying wagons and thunder
they rumble through us and are gone.

Fall's Labor, Fall's Memory

Suppose this day of clearing
is a room I'll forget in ten years,
but for an image or two—Will it be
red-orange leaves cindering

the stoop, boots wet with dew
drying on the sidewalk, leaking
small shadows at their heels?
Light knits together twig

and inchworm, brushes my hand
as it sweats. I pry up rocks from clay,
and hope I'll recall the heat
between arm and shovel, a goodness

of work sparking between steel
and flint. This time of year, people
burn in barrels, smoke the air
with old things they've let go.

But we never really know
what we'll long for later, whose face
might flutter down a scaffold
of color. There are questions

I'd ask my dad if he were still alive,
he'd pause with his rake and say,
well, let me think now . . . . . .
then would, as best he could, remember.

Morning After Rain

It's a half mile walk in woods
to find the creek recharged,
to feel spidery trails on arms
but more than that, to hear
in second rain from wind-shed
trees, a purer refrain of water,
the law of a droplet tapping five leaves
before cascading bitterweed
to fern, moss to river stone—
as a life might trickle down
in diamond streams if you let it.
It's possible to find a place here,
small cloudbursts of peace
mists that filter past the skin
to all dry prisons held inside,
each cell replaced with acres
of gravity and slow turning.
Life lends itself along the banks
in iron, copper, or sun—
compositions we don't know
but in time, swim inside us.

Winter Vultures

They may be the only creatures
who don't go hungry
in winter, fat on delicacies

of possum, the plenitude
of belly-up flesh
on frozen grass. Their shadows

swoop rounds on hay
seeming to chase each other
as a child and her father's will

when she rides atop
his shoulders late afternoon
a tiny dark bird perched

weightless, black notes floating
above. Deep blue images
of the pair blend on bare ground

rendering a song of sky
the two cannot hear in their earth
trance, music of a moment

they will forget and leave behind,
to be plucked clean
on the cold twilight fields.

The Morning My Father Is Buried

It is early November
a first breath of frost tarps
the grave white as a bible
slicking the incline where six

men stagger to keep purchase
on our family plot, coffin
sealed and shouldered.
They are so careful of you,

of leaves that want to play
with our mourning, unseat it
to a tumble. I know how drab
my grief is next to this mountain,

have seen waters gearing
down it, how its blaze rares up
in autumn, spits when a drop
of rain hits, acres of red-gold

fed by the flint of the dead.
It isn't death's wound, but the snap
of steel that locks you in
a hymn sung in metal notes

sunk in the ore of women's voices.
I see you banging a spoon
on Sunday morning to wake us up.
If I lean in, my shadow leans

in toward you as you fall.
It's that other world we must believe
in, where lowered to a native
land, rivers can shout, praise come.

From Ice and Dust

All summer long a comet
streaks, star-blown and cold
as I walk, hollow-boned
thin-ribbed, a scarecrow loosed

upon the night trailing cotton.
How elastic the hands once,
thick with boxwood and petunias,
a face blankly ignorant

of kneecaps and hips, their gray
aching moonscape. From the closet
of sky, original dust returns,
its tiny solid planet flashes

the same blinkered path always,
a brightness not consuming
itself, a body falling, falling
for miles, whole and unbroken.

Blackbird Days

There must be upwards
of five hundred grackle in the trees
shadow hats along limbs
crackling choruses of evil-eye
if lore holds sway, always
a human face looking up
wondering what kind of cold
will come. November offers signs
to be read, like some nomadic
youth we've put aside,
they drop wing upon wing
eclipsing branches, bits of tinsel
in the mouth, flashing certainty
in what has pulled us by wind,
one place to another.
Older now, the heart reshuffles
in twilight, akilter in the boughs,
our blackbird days
peering into a dark unknown,
finding it iridescent.

About the Author

Sharon Perkins Ackerman is an Appalachian poet living near the Blue Ridge of central Virginia.

Her poems have appeared in *The Southern Humanities Review, Atlanta Review, Appalachian Places, Valparaiso Poetry Review, Roanoke Review, Meridian, Still: The Journal, Salvation South, Blue Mountain Review,* and various other places.

She is the winner of the Hippocrates Prize for Poetry, London, 2019. She has one poetry collection, *Revised Light* (Main Street Rag, 2021) and works as poetry editor for *Streetlight Magazine*.

www.ingramcontent.com/pod-product-compliance
Lightning Source LLC
Chambersburg PA
CBHW070937160426
43193CB00011B/1719